Praise For No More Dancing

"*No More Dancing is a masterful blend of personal storytelling, evidence-based insights, and practical strategies. Carlos J. Malave's use of dance as a metaphor for avoiding hard conversations is both powerful and eye-opening, challenging readers to embrace necessary change. This book is essential for leaders, educators, and changemakers looking to foster inclusivity, transform workplace culture, and create environments where individuals feel valued and heard.*"

- Raymona H. Lawrence, DrPH, MPH, CDE®
- Georgia Southern University Professor

"*Carlos J. Malave's courage in using his own life as a model for learning makes No More Dancing extraordinary. From the beats of Salsa, Merengue, and Bachata to his realizations about 'dancing around' difficult emotions, his journey is a testament to raw honesty and transformation. This book blends personal experience with practical wisdom, offering both heart and strategy for those seeking authentic living and meaningful change.*"

- Dr. Nathaniel Bouie, High School Administrator

"*Having known Carlos since childhood, I've witnessed his transformation into a powerful voice for truth and authenticity. No More Dancing dismantles the habit of avoidance with raw honesty and compelling storytelling, offering a* roadmap to courageous conversations. If you're ready to stop sidestepping hard truths and build deeper, more authentic connections, this book is for you."

- **Dr. Cheyenne Ray, PhD, Corporate HR Strategist**

"Inspiring, urgent, and deeply personal, No More Dancing is a powerful call to action. Carlos J. Malave's before-and-after framework brilliantly illustrates transformation in real time, making this more than just an emotional read—it's a manifesto for authentic change, healing, and connection."

- **Dr. Terainer Brown, Higher Education Scholar-Practitioner**

"*No More Dancing* hit me in a way I didn't expect—it reflects the battles we all face but rarely talk about. Carlos J. Malave doesn't sugarcoat the truth; he makes you sit with it, feel it, and ultimately face it. This book isn't about perfection—it's about progress, choosing healing over avoidance, and truth over comfort. Thank you, Carlos, for saving the last dance—not for avoidance, but for freedom and self-discovery."

- **Kenneth Scott, RICE University Professor**

"In No More Dancing, Carlos J. Malave captures the struggle of suppressing our truth for the comfort of others. This book made me feel seen and validated, reminding me that authenticity should never be sacrificed. More than just insight, it *provides the intentional work needed to turn awareness into transformative change."*

— **Alex Gay, Middle School Administrator**

"No More Dancing confronts a truth many of us avoid— we dance around honesty out of fear of confrontation, disappointment, or judgment. Carlos J. Malave challenges us to step out of the shadows, embrace difficult conversations, and choose restoration over avoidance. His message is especially powerful for those who have spent years holding it all in. This book is a call to freedom through truth."

— **Frederick Keenan, College Professor**

"No More Dancing is a raw, powerful page-turner that captures the essence of 'keeping it real.' Carlos J. Malave dismantles the myth of machismo and offers a blueprint for confronting avoidance and fear. His storytelling challenged me to examine my own reluctance to face unspoken truths—an essential read for anyone ready to break free from emotional silence."

— **Christopher Rose, High School Administrator**

"No More Dancing beautifully explores how generational trauma can be broken through the power of restorative living. Carlos J. Malave offers a touching homage to his father, wife, and daughter, showing how empathy, clarity, and accountability strengthen our connections. This

book is a powerful guide to holding difficult conversations, setting healthy boundaries, and empowering those we care for to do the same."

> - **Dr. Amarilys Estrella, Professor of Anthropology, Rice University**

"No More Dancing isn't just a book—it's a wake-up call. Carlos J. Malave doesn't just write about breaking cycles; he walks you through them with truth, vulnerability, and wisdom that make you pause mid-page to reflect. This book pushed me to stop performing, start healing, and embrace the freedom that comes from living in truth. A game-changer."

> - **Jeremiah Brown, Former NFL Athlete, Speaker & Mental Health Advocate**

"No More Dancing is a call to action. Carlos J. Malave challenges us to stop avoiding tough conversations and instead embrace deeper, more authentic connections. Through personal narrative and actionable steps, he shows us how to strengthen our relationships—both with others and ourselves—by honoring boundaries and speaking our truth."

> - **Chris Nuñez, LMSW, Case Management Director at Rice University**

"As a father and son, I admire the courage it took to write No More Dancing. Turning pain into healing is a rare gift, and Carlos J. Malave is one of the few who does it masterfully. This book is both a testimony to his strength and a powerful reminder that our struggles can either break us or make us. Maintain perseverance and align yourself with the life you desire."

- **Darin 'BuddieRoe' Venters, Hip Hop Artist**

"No More Dancing provides a blueprint for transforming personal pain into collective healing. Carlos J. Malave challenges us to stop running from hard truths and step into the peace that comes with living intentionally. A must-read for anyone ready to break cycles, set boundaries, and build a life rooted in truth and restoration."

- **David J. Crawford, College Administrator**

NO MORE DANCING

Embracing the Power of Restorative Living

CARLOS J. MALAVE

Copyright @ 2025 by Carlos Malave
Cover Design: Tri Widyatmaka
Interior Design: Tri Widyatmaka

All rights reserved. No part of this publication may be reproduced, used, performed, stored in a retrieval system, or transmitted in any form or by any means, electronic, mechanical, photocopying, recording, or otherwise, without the prior written permission of the author, Carlos Malave, if living, except for critical articles or reviews.

The author of this book does not dispense health or medical advice, only offers information of a general nature to help you in your quest for maximum success. This book is not designed to be a definitive guide or to take the place of advice from a qualified professional, and there is no guarantee that the methods suggested in this book will be successful, owing to the risk that is involved in any journey of life. Thus, neither the publisher nor the author assumes liability for any losses that may be sustained by the use of the methods described in this book, and any such liability is hereby expressly disclaimed. In the event you use any of the information in this book for yourself, the author and the publisher assume no responsibility for your actions.

1st edition, May 2025 ISBN-13: 979-8-218-66380-3
Printed in the United States of America

CONTENTS

The Last Letter xv

Introduction xvii
Embracing the Dance of Boundaries xvii

Chapter One
The Burden of Unspoken Truths 1

Chapter Two
Breaking Free 9

Chapter Three
Restorative Power 20

Chapter Four
The Power of Alignment 28

Chapter Five
The F Word 37

Chapter Six
Building Community 47

Chapter Seven
Legacy 57

Chapter Eight
Conclusion: Embracing the Power of Restorative Living   69

> ***Reflections in Pictures*** 83
> ***Acknowledgments*** 87
> ***References*** 89
> ***About the Author*** 91

"Your peace is non-negotiable. Prioritize yourself, for when you honor your own comfort, you create the space to truly show up for others—authentic, whole, and unbroken."

Dedicated to the Life of my Father Carlos R. Malave
December 2, 1964- January 12, 2019

"Though you're no longer with me in the physical world, a part of you lives on in me—your spirit, your strength, your love. I carry you with me every day, in everything I do, and I know you're always with me in a way that's beyond words."

THE LAST LETTER

Dear Pa,

I've been thinking a lot about you lately—about the man you were and the father you became, despite not having a clear roadmap or the role models you needed to guide you. You carved your own path, and in doing so, you shaped me into the person I am today. No one told you how to do it, but you figured it out with determination and love, and I can't begin to express how grateful I am for that.

I know sometimes your methods might have seemed a little unconventional—maybe even a bit wacko at times—but you never gave up on me. You stayed on my behind, pushing me to be better, to reach higher, and, most importantly, to believe in myself. You made sure I knew I was capable of anything, but also that the world wasn't always going to be kind. You protected me from it and gave me the space to dream. And even though you were hard on me at times, I always felt your love underneath it all.

I'll never forget what you once told me—that I was the man you wished to be. But Pa, the truth is, I'm just a reflection of the light you shone on me every single day. Your kindness, your vulnerability, and your unwavering honesty—those are the qualities that made me who I am. Yes, you had your flaws. We all do. But failure wasn't what I saw in you. What I saw was your relentless effort to grow, to learn, and to be better, even when life wasn't easy. And that—your commitment to growth and self-improvement—is what has made me who I am today.

I don't think you'll ever truly understand just how powerful you've made me. I'm not perfect, but I am strong, and I am capable because you were there, showing me the way, every step of the way. Man, I'm so proud of you. I can't even put it into words.

Thank you for staying true to yourself. Thanks for being my dad, loving me, and teaching me to be a man. I am who I am because of you—and I will carry that with me for the rest of my life.

Pa, I love you. Always have. Always will.

With all my heart,
Your Firstborn,
Carlito

INTRODUCTION

Embracing the Dance of Boundaries

"Dancing around the truth doesn't just delay the inevitable—it destroys lives. It's what killed my father, and it's what's killing so many others today. The time for sidestepping hard conversations is over."

We live in a world where avoidance has become second nature. The pandemic, in particular, reinforced a new normal of disconnection. We got used to muting ourselves—literally and figuratively—on Zoom calls, avoiding eye contact behind masks, and keeping our distance, both physically and emotionally. In many ways, it was as if we were all at a silent party, each of us with headphones on, in the same space but hearing different things, moving in rhythm yet never truly connecting. And now, even though life has resumed, the habit of avoidance lingers. We dance around difficult conversations, sidestepping them with small talk, scrolling past them on our screens, or burying them under the guise of "keeping the peace."

Growing up, the rhythm of my life was shaped by the music that played around me. Salsa, Merengue, Bachata—these were not just dances; they were languages. In my childhood home, the pulse of the beat dictated how we moved, how we connected, and how we communicated. When the music started, it felt like everyone around me was invited to participate. With each sway of the hips, each twist of the body, a sense of unity and understanding emerged. It was instinctive; no one questioned it, and no one hesitated. The dance was a conversation. A dialogue where emotions, experiences, and expectations could be expressed without words.

But here's the thing: life is not just a dance.

In the same way that people flow to the rhythm of the music, I had learned to "dance around" my own issues, avoiding uncomfortable truths and direct confrontation. I danced around problems in relationships, masked my discomfort with the beats of politeness, and sidestepped difficult conversations for the sake of keeping the peace. I became so good at it that, for a long time, I didn't even recognize how much of myself I was losing in the process.

But the truth, as it often does, has a way of catching up with us. There comes a point when the music stops. There comes a time when the constant motion and avoidance no longer serve us. For me, that moment came with a simple realization: dancing around my issues was no longer a healthy choice. And so, I embarked on a journey—a journey of learning to set boundaries, to prioritize my emotional health, and to embrace discomfort for the sake of real, meaningful connections.

That journey hasn't been flawless, but it has been transformative. Old habits don't disappear overnight, and I'd be lying if I said I never catch myself slipping into people-pleasing or sidestepping hard conversations. But the difference now is that I recognize those moments for what they are: opportunities to choose growth over comfort. Each time I lean into the discomfort instead of avoiding it, I see how honest dialogue strengthens trust, how clear boundaries foster respect, and how standing firm in my values creates the connection I once feared losing.

This book isn't written from a pedestal of perfection, but it's not written from square one either. This book represents the culmination of hard-earned lessons, practical strategies, and the kind of growth that can only be achieved through hard work. I'm sharing what's helped me move from avoidance to authenticity—not as someone who's mastered it all, but as someone who's made meaningful progress and is committed to helping others do the same. I hope that you'll find both encouragement and actionable steps here—proof that imperfect progress is not just possible but powerful.

Why This Book is Urgent

We live in a time where avoidance is easier than ever. Social media allows us to curate our lives, showing only what we want people to see. Cancel culture punishes mistakes without dialogue. Fear of discomfort drives us to silence instead of solutions. We send texts instead of making phone calls, ghost people instead of addressing conflict, and suppress our feelings rather than express them. The result? Despite being more "connected" than ever, the result is fractured relationships, unspoken pain, and an increasingly disconnected society.

We are dancing around the truth in ways that are eroding the very foundation of our personal and professional relationships. And the cost is staggering.

When we refuse to engage in the hard conversations, we leave wounds unhealed and problems unresolved, allowing them to fester until they explode—or worse, quietly corrode everything we value most.

That's why this book matters.

This journey isn't just about communication; it's about survival. It's about breaking the cycle of avoidance before it destroys more lives, more relationships, and more futures. The hard conversations we avoid today could be the very thing that unlocks more profound understanding, stronger connections, and lasting change.

This book is your invitation to step into those moments with courage. This book encourages you to cease your dancing and begin taking action. When we choose to confront the hard truths with the right energy—an energy of empathy, clarity, and accountability—we not only transform our own lives but also create a ripple effect that affects everyone around us.

The Personal Cost of Avoidance

For me, the habit of avoidance was learned early. Direct confrontation was uncommon in my family. My family diffused arguments with humor, buried tension under distractions, and often sacrificed honesty to maintain peace. The unspoken rule was clear: some things were just better left unsaid.

At school, I perfected this skill. If I was upset with a friend, I buried it. If I was hurt, I laughed it off. People liked me because I was easygoing and agreeable, but underneath the surface, resentment quietly brewed.

I remember one moment in high school when a close friend borrowed something of mine and never returned it. I was frustrated but didn't say a word. Months later, I snapped over something trivial, and our friendship was never the same. That moment taught me that avoidance doesn't just delay conflict—it distorts it.

In adulthood, this pattern persisted. I avoided hard conversations with coworkers, friends, and even loved ones. My desire to keep things smooth often meant sacrificing my own needs or feelings. But what I didn't realize was that my silence wasn't just protecting others—it was hurting me. It was eroding my self-esteem, limiting my growth, and creating barriers in my relationships.

The Role of Empathy in Confrontation

Breaking free from the dance of avoidance requires a willingness to embrace discomfort. This doesn't mean seeking out conflict but rather facing it with courage and clarity when it arises. It's about valuing honesty over harmony and long-term connection over short-term ease.

One of the most impactful lessons I've learned is that discomfort is temporary, but the growth it brings can be transformative. I remember a conversation with a close friend who had unknowingly hurt me. I was terrified to bring it up, fearing it would ruin our friendship. But when I finally did, the outcome surprised me. Not only did it strengthen our bond, but it also taught me that vulnerability is a bridge, not a barrier.

Empathy is the cornerstone of healthy confrontation. When we approach difficult conversations with the intent to understand rather than to win, we create space for mutual growth. This shift in perspective can turn a potentially divisive moment into an opportunity for connection.

I've seen this firsthand in my work. One client shared how a simple practice of active listening—repeating back what the other person said to ensure understanding—completely changed their dynamic with their teenage son. Instead of arguments, they had dialogues. Instead of walls, they built bridges.

The Ripple Effect of Facing Hard Truths

When we choose to confront hard truths, the impact extends far beyond ourselves. It influences our families, communities, and even workplaces. Leaders who address issues head-on inspire trust and foster a culture of accountability. Parents who model honest communication teach their children the value of authenticity. Friends who set boundaries create healthier, more fulfilling relationships built on mutual respect.

This ripple effect begins small but grows with every act of courage. When one person chooses to address conflict constructively, it sends a message to others that honesty, though uncomfortable, is worth it. It empowers people to speak their truths, take ownership of their actions, and approach challenges with clarity and compassion.

Imagine a world where difficult conversations are met with courage instead of avoidance. Picture this: A young woman, once weighed down by years of unresolved tension, walks out of a workshop with a sense of clarity she didn't know she needed. Inspired by the principles of "no more dancing around the issue," she sits down with her father that evening.

At first, the words come slowly, carefully, as they both navigate a topic they've long avoided. But then, something shifts. Her vulnerability unlocks his honesty, and for the first time, they see each other's perspectives clearly. They laugh, they cry, and most importantly, they plan a way forward—together.

What was once a silent, growing chasm between them becomes a bridge of understanding and hope.

A Call to Action

No More Dancing isn't just about confronting issues; it's about transforming relationships, healing wounds, and creating a legacy of connection for generations to come.

This book serves as your guide, not from someone who has perfected every challenging conversation, but from someone who has discovered through experience that avoidance is never the solution. My journey is ongoing, just like yours. But if there's one thing I've learned, it's this: The truth is always worth facing.

The choice to stop dancing around the truth is not just a personal decision; it's a commitment to creating a world where authenticity and connection reign. Each step forward inspires others to do the same, proving that the courage to confront is not just transformative—it's contagious.

And that, perhaps, is the greatest gift we can offer: the example of a life lived in truth, sparking change in ways we may never fully see but can always trust will grow.

CHAPTER ONE

The Burden of Unspoken Truths

There was a boy I knew, a boy who wore his burdens like a cloak—heavy and suffocating. His heart was pure, and his intentions were good, but life seemed determined to test him at every turn. I watched him grow, not just physically, but emotionally—though sometimes it felt like he was stuck, suspended in the weight of his experiences, never quite able to escape the shadows of his past.

Like many of us, this boy had a lot on his plate. He was young, yet his life was already complicated, filled with things no child should have to carry. He didn't grow up with much, and the little he had often came with the sting of poverty. He struggled with holes in his shoes, clothes that never fit perfectly, and a constant reminder that his desires didn't always align with his financial means. But these were the least of his worries.

Before his father passed away, the memories the boy had of him were far from what a child should look back on with warmth. He remembered the fights. The yelling. His father drunk, angry, and distant. He remembered the shame of seeing his mother take the brunt of it, her strength as evident as her silence. She didn't speak much—especially about the pain. She just carried it, silently. And the boy, unsure of how to handle the chaos, learned to carry it too.

But it wasn't just his parents' struggles that affected him. The boy had siblings—brothers and sisters he loved and cared for. He found solace in their company, a brief reprieve from the tension at home. But even in his moments of peace, he couldn't escape the harsh reality of the world around him. He witnessed his older sisters being verbally and physically abused by their partners. He saw his older brothers, in the wake of their father's passing, step up as the men of the house. But instead of providing structure, they unknowingly became part of the cycle of trauma, using discipline as a shield for their own unresolved pain.

This boy's story isn't unique. Research from the Substance Abuse and Mental Health Services Administration (SAMHSA) reveals that more than two-thirds of children experience at least one traumatic event before the age of 16. These events—domestic violence, poverty, substance abuse, or neglect—have a profound impact on mental and emotional well-being, often following individuals well into adulthood. As Peter Levine, trauma expert and author, aptly states, "Trauma is a fact of life. It does not, however, have to be a life sentence."

However, for this boy, trauma felt inescapable. The most dangerous part was that, like many kids in toxic environments, he was taught that the outside world had no right to know the truth. He learned the cardinal rule: "What happens at home, stays at home." While this might seem like a reasonable boundary to some, it became his prison. He had no outlet, no safe space to express his pain, no one to listen—only the weight of unspoken truths.

NO MORE DANCING

This mentality, though deeply ingrained, became a dangerous trap. Studies published in Psychology Today emphasize how cultural norms—especially those rooted in traditional masculinity—teach boys to suppress their emotions, equating vulnerability with weakness. The boy learned this lesson early. It taught him to suppress his emotions, avoid confronting the chaos at home, and keep the mask of normalcy firmly in place. Without an outlet for his emotions, the pressure began to build up. He couldn't focus. He couldn't concentrate. He couldn't enjoy his childhood.

And so, one day, during a class at school, his distractions finally caught the attention of his teacher. In front of the whole class, she called him out, questioning his lack of focus. The boy, already embarrassed by his inner turmoil, couldn't contain it. His defense mechanism kicked in. He lashed out—not just at his teacher, but at his classmates. A single glance from one of his male classmates triggered something deep inside him. He couldn't let anyone see the truth. If his classmate could see the hurt behind his eyes—the vulnerability trying to break through— then he would be weak. And weakness meant ridicule, rejection, and more pain.

This moment is not an isolated incident but rather a reflection of a systemic issue seen in classrooms across the country. Research from the National Center for Education Statistics highlights that approximately 13% of students in public schools receive disciplinary actions such as suspensions or expulsions annually, many stemming from behavioral outbursts linked to underlying emotional struggles. Furthermore, studies published in the Journal of School Psychology reveal that students experiencing adverse childhood experiences (ACEs) are significantly more likely to exhibit disruptive behavior in class. These children, often misunderstood, are labeled as troublemakers rather than being seen as individuals in need of support and understanding.

Instead of allowing that moment of vulnerability to surface, the boy masked it with anger. He stared back, his eyes filled with defiance, and in a burst of emotion, he shouted, "WHAT ARE YOU LOOKING AT!" The classroom erupted in chaos. A fight broke out. And the cycle continued.

Such incidents highlight the profound impact of teacher responses on students. A study from the Collaborative for Academic, Social, and Emotional Learning (CASEL) underscores the importance of fostering emotional intelligence in educators. Teachers who are trained to recognize and address emotional triggers in students can defuse situations like this before they escalate. However, without adequate training, many educators react out of frustration or confusion, inadvertently reinforcing the cycle of shame and anger in vulnerable children.

As the boy grew older, he became more accustomed to hiding his emotions behind walls of anger and defensiveness. Society demanded he be tough—strong, silent, and unwavering. But inside, he was breaking. The pain, the trauma, the unresolved emotions—it all began to manifest in ways he didn't know how to handle. He sought solace in other ways: the gym, where he could channel his anger into strength; alcohol, which numbed the ache that had no name; and distractions from the truth quietly eating him alive.

The boy's experience mirrors findings from the Centers for Disease Control and Prevention (CDC), which indicate that children who lack emotional support systems are more likely to develop coping mechanisms that include substance abuse, aggression, and academic underachievement. The American Psychological Association further reports that punitive measures, like public reprimands or suspensions, often exacerbate these behaviors instead of addressing the root causes. These statistics paint a sobering picture: the cycle of emotional suppression and misbehavior continues unless intentional interventions are made.

To break this cycle, schools must prioritize trauma-informed practices. Programs like Positive Behavioral Interventions and Supports (PBIS) and restorative justice have shown promise in reducing disciplinary issues while fostering a culture of empathy and understanding. For example, a study by the University of California, Berkeley, found that implementing restorative practices led to a 43% reduction in suspensions and an increase in overall academic performance. Such approaches empower both educators and students to address conflicts constructively, creating an environment where vulnerability is not punished but supported.

Moments like the one this boy faced occur all too often in schools, underscoring the urgent need for systemic change. It is not enough to discipline without understanding; we must create spaces where students feel safe to express their pain without fear of ridicule or rejection. This transformation requires collective effort—from educators, administrators, and policymakers—to ensure that no child bears the weight of unspoken truths alone.

Years passed, and the boy became a man. He married, had children, and became a hardworking union employee. On the surface, he seemed to have it all together. But deep down, he was still running—running from the unresolved pain of his past, from the trauma he never learned to process. He added responsibilities to his life, thinking that by doing so, he could outrun his demons.

But all he did was bury them deeper, and with every new role he took on, the pressure grew heavier. The weight of his own unresolved feelings began to suffocate him.

When conflict came, as it always does, he didn't know how to handle it. He didn't know how to communicate his emotions. He didn't know how to be vulnerable without feeling like he was failing. So, he withdrew. He self-destructed. And in the process, he hurt the very people he loved the most—his wife, his children, and his friends. The relationships, which should have been sources of strength, became casualties of his unresolved trauma.

The boy, now a man, reached a critical moment. He understood that something needed to shift. He wanted to be better, to be the kind of father and husband his family could be proud of. But there was a problem: he wasn't doing it for himself. He was trying to change to please others, to earn their approval. And that, as we all know, is a recipe for failure. When we do things for others and not for ourselves, we are doomed to repeat the same cycles of self-sabotage.

In the end, despite his efforts, the boy-turned-man couldn't escape his inner turmoil. On January 10th, 2019, Carlos Ruben Malave, the man who had been my father, my role model, and my inspiration, took his own life.

This is my why.

Carlos's story, and so many like it, serves as a testament to the damage caused by a culture that discourages vulnerability and emotional honesty, especially in men. His story doesn't have to end in tragedy. It's the reason I've created the Restorative Power Curriculum and this book: to help children and adults alike learn to process their emotions, confront their trauma, and break the cycles of pain passed down from generation to generation.

As UNC researchers have pointed out, "The trauma is held personally and transmitted over generations." But the cycle can stop with us. It starts with understanding. It starts with vulnerability. It starts with rewriting the narrative.

It starts with you.

Action Steps

What do you know about Restorative Practice?

_____

_____

_____

_____

_____

If it is something used within your community, then how does it work? And, if it isn't used within your community, then how can you see Restorative Practices being useful?

_____

_____

_____

_____

_____

Do you believe Restorative Practices can be used as lifestyle practices? Why or why not?

_____
_____
_____
_____
_____

CHAPTER TWO

Breaking Free

What is the weight of growing up too fast?

Have you ever carried a burden you weren't prepared for, such as the unspoken expectation of being everyone's rock or being the oldest child responsible for your siblings?

The Impact of Early Responsibility and Emotional Burden

Children who grow up too quickly due to familial or societal pressures often face long-term consequences. According to the *American Psychological Association (APA)*, "parentification"—a term used to describe children taking on adult responsibilities—has been linked to chronic stress, anxiety, and difficulties in forming healthy relationships later in life. A study in *The Journal of Child Psychology and Psychiatry* found that parentified children are at greater risk for depression and emotional dysregulation as adults, stemming from a premature loss of childhood innocence.

For my father, the weight of disappointment and trauma rewired how he saw the world—and himself. It wasn't until my teenage years, driven by curiosity, that I started asking him real questions. The stories that spilled out changed everything.

The Role of Trauma in Mental Health

The Centers for Disease Control and Prevention (CDC) reports that adverse childhood experiences (ACEs), such as poverty, parental mental illness, and exposure to violence, increase the likelihood of mental health issues in adulthood. My father's experiences—walking barefoot to school in Puerto Rico, fighting gangs in New York, and holding down a labor-intensive job—were his ACEs. These shaped his resilience but also left him emotionally scarred.

Barriers to Seeking Help

Facing the realities that my father went through was not something he was open to doing. Like many others who looked like my dad, there was a disillusionment with therapy. Studies show that minority populations are 20% less likely to access mental health services due to systemic barriers, cultural stigma, and mistrust in healthcare systems (*National Alliance on Mental Illness*). This mistrust often results in people turning to family members or self-reliance for emotional support, which can unintentionally overburden their loved ones.

For years, my father seemed like a prisoner to his own mind, shackled by thoughts he couldn't escape. I'd watch him wrestle with his worries and tell him, "Pa, you think too much. Just chill." He'd always respond, "I know, but I can't. I'm not like you guys. My mind works differently." And it did—only I didn't understand why.

What happens when someone carries more than they were ever designed to hold? Imagine lifting a weight far beyond your capacity. It doesn't just strain you in the moment; it reshapes your body, warps your posture, and leaves you with invisible scars. For my father, the weight of disappointment and trauma rewired how he saw the world—and himself.

It wasn't until my teenage years, driven by curiosity, that I started asking him real questions. The stories that spilled out changed everything. We would sit for hours, peeling back the layers of his life: his childhood struggles, his wild ambition, the sacrifices he made, and the weight of his disappointments.

He shared how he once walked barefoot to school in Puerto Rico and arrived in New York City with nothing but a dream. He faced thugs and gangs in his neighborhood, but through sheer grit, he built a life with a college-educated wife, raised three children, and held the same construction job for 25 years. My father was a fighter, but beneath his resilience was a weight he could never set down.

The weight of growing up too fast. Can you relate? Were you thrust into responsibilities you weren't ready for? Maybe you were the protector in your family, the one everyone turned to for comfort. Maybe you sacrificed your childhood or teenage years because someone else needed you to be strong. How does that affect a person? When you're forced to carry weight prematurely, it stunts your growth—not just physically, but emotionally and spiritually.

For my father, his mind was haunted by traumas he never addressed. My mother encouraged him to try therapy, but after a few sessions, he came home disillusioned. "They don't tell me anything," he said. "They don't give me answers." So, he stopped going.

Have you ever tried something that didn't work the first time and given up? Therapy is one of those things. Healing rarely happens instantly—it's a process that requires patience. It's like a gift that comes without batteries. You have the potential to experience its benefits, but only if you put in the effort to make it work.

In my youthful arrogance, I believed my father. I thought I could be what he needed—someone who understood him without judgment. But here's the truth: What happens when the weight you're carrying isn't yours?

For years, I became his confidant, the person he leaned on for clarity and comfort. It brought us closer, but it also made me his emotional lifeline. I took pride in that role, but as I started my family, the strain of being both son and counselor became overwhelming. I had to step back for my own mental health. And while I knew it was the right decision, it wasn't easy.

Our once-deep conversations faded, replaced by silence. Then, on October 17, 2018, everything changed. While teaching at KIPP Houston High School, I got a call from my father. I could hear the roar of the subway in the background as he said, "I'm sorry. I can't handle it anymore. I'm going to jump."

My world froze. Desperately, I stayed on the line, talking him down until he promised to be okay. By the end of the call, we had a plan to move forward, but the weight of that moment broke me.

"Why me?" I asked my wife later that night. "Why couldn't we just have a normal father-son relationship?"

What do you do when the person who was supposed to protect you starts leaning on you instead? It's a question many people have to wrestle with. If you've ever been in that situation, you understand the emotional toll it takes. There's a quiet grief in having to grow up too fast— in losing the space to just be.

The following months were a balancing act—supporting my father while managing my own life. When he took his own life in 2019, I was left with a profound void. My wife, seeing my grief, asked me a question that changed everything:

"Now that your father—the man you've measured yourself against your whole life—is gone, do you know who you want to be?"

Her question forced me to confront the identity I had built around my father's shadow. It also made me realize something else: the power of questions. A single, well-placed question can be a lifeline. It can cut through the noise and force you to examine the truth.

Looking back, I could have dismissed her question as insensitive or poorly timed. But I didn't. Why? Because our relationship had been built on trust, vulnerability, and hard conversations. When you have someone in your life who can ask you the tough questions, it's a gift.

Her question became the spark I needed to start a new journey. Therapy, which I had once dismissed like my dad did, became not just an option but a necessity.

Struggles with Therapy and Finding the Right Fit

At first, finding the right therapist felt impossible. I almost gave up, but eventually, I found someone who felt like a fit. Therapy wasn't about getting answers; it was about releasing the burdens I had carried for too long.

The process of finding the right therapist can be overwhelming, especially for people who have never sought mental health support before. Studies show that nearly **50% of individuals who start therapy drop out after the first session (Journal** *of Counseling Psychology*). This high dropout rate is often due to barriers such as a lack of cultural competence, financial constraints, or the absence of a strong therapeutic connection.

For marginalized communities, these challenges are compounded. The *American Psychological Association (APA)* notes that only **22% of Black adults and 25% of Hispanic adults with mental health conditions receive treatment**, compared to 40% of white adults. Reasons for this disparity include cultural stigma, lack of representation among therapists, and mistrust in the healthcare system.

NO MORE DANCING

Therapy Isn't Linear

Have you ever carried a weight so long you forgot it was there? Therapy helped me put that weight down. It didn't fix me because I wasn't broken—but it helped me understand myself in ways I never thought possible.

This experience isn't unique. Therapy often feels nonlinear because healing itself is nonlinear. The *National Alliance on Mental Illness (NAMI)* emphasizes that recovery is a journey, not a destination. A 2020 study in the *Journal of Affective Disorders* revealed that clients often experience "relapses" in emotional pain during therapy, but these moments are part of a broader pattern of growth and self-awareness.

Therapy also reminded me of something crucial: healing isn't linear. It's messy, unpredictable, and often uncomfortable. But it's worth it.

Historical Misuse of Therapy and Mental Health Practices Against People of Color For people of color, therapy comes with a fraught history. Mental health practices have historically been weaponized against marginalized communities, contributing to the deep mistrust many feel toward the mental health system today.

1. **Pathologizing Blackness**

   During the 19th century, pseudoscientific diagnoses like "drapetomania" were invented to justify the oppression of enslaved Black people. This so-called "mental illness" described enslaved individuals' desire to escape bondage as a psychiatric disorder. (*American Journal of Psychiatry,* *2020*).

2. **Experimentation and Abuse**

   Throughout the 20th century, Black and Brown communities were disproportionately targeted for unethical experiments, such as the *Tuskegee Syphilis Study*, where Black men were denied treatment for syphilis under the guise of research. These abuses extended to mental health, where marginalized groups were often subject to invasive treatments like lobotomies at higher rates (*National Library of Medicine*).

3. **Overdiagnosis and Misdiagnosis**

   Studies have shown that Black and Hispanic individuals are more likely to be misdiagnosed with schizophrenia and other severe mental health conditions compared to their white counterparts, even when presenting the same symptoms (*Journal of Clinical Psychiatry, 2017*). This misdiagnosis often stems from systemic biases and a lack of cultural competence among mental health professionals.

4. **Cultural Mistrust**

   These historical abuses have led to cultural mistrust—a protective mechanism that can make seeking therapy feel unsafe or counterproductive. According to a 2021 study published in *Social Psychiatry and Psychiatric Epidemiology*, cultural mistrust significantly reduces the likelihood of Black Americans seeking mental health treatment, even when they have access to it.

Addressing the Challenges

To address these systemic barriers, mental health organizations are advocating for reforms such as

- **Increasing Representation**: Less than **4% of psychologists in the U.S. are Black**, despite Black people making up 13% of the population (*APA*). Efforts to diversify the mental health workforce aim to bridge this gap.
- **Culturally Relevant Therapy Models**: Approaches like *Culturally Adapted Cognitive Behavioral Therapy (CA-CBT)* have been shown to improve outcomes for people of color by integrating cultural values and lived experiences into treatment (*Clinical Psychology Review, 2019*).
- **Community-Based Initiatives**: Grassroots programs like *Therapy for Black Girls* and *The Boris Lawrence Henson Foundation* are making therapy more accessible by providing culturally competent care and reducing financial barriers.

A Call to Action

Therapy should not feel like an impossible journey or an unwelcoming space, but for many, it still does. The weight of systemic inequities and historical injustices has made mental health care feel inaccessible to entire communities. However, change is happening.

If you're struggling to find the right therapist, don't give up. Look for therapists who are trained in cultural competence or specialize in your specific needs. Resources like *Psychology Today*, *Inclusive Therapists*, and *Open Path Collective* can help you find affordable and culturally relevant options.

Healing may not be linear, but it is possible. Therapy isn't just about putting down the weight—it's about understanding how that weight shaped you and choosing how you want to move forward.

What would your life look like if you stopped carrying everyone else's weight?

Action Steps

1. Reflect on your beliefs about therapy.

    What were you told about therapy growing up? How did those beliefs shape your views on seeking help?

2. Evaluate your perspective on therapy today.

    Do you feel the same way now? Why or why not? What experiences or people have influenced your current view?

3. Consider therapy as an option for you.

    Is therapy something you're open to? Why or why not? What are the barriers or motivations driving that decision?

Reflection Quote

"True strength comes from learning to release, not just to hold. Therapy can be that release—a place to lay down the weight and start again."

CHAPTER THREE

Restorative Power

Restoration has always been more powerful than punishment. While consequences might force compliance, only restoration can heal the harm beneath the surface. This truth isn't new. Long before modern systems formalized restorative practices, communities around the world embraced them as a way to mend relationships, not just enforce rules.

Across cultures and centuries, the emphasis has been the same: when harm occurs, the goal isn't to isolate the offender but to restore trust, accountability, and connection. In traditional Zulu society, for example, justice was never about retribution. Instead, offenders were required to make amends, not just with the individual they harmed but with the community as a whole. This approach didn't just resolve the immediate conflict; it reinforced relationships and strengthened the social fabric.

Similarly, the Maori people of New Zealand have long practiced restorative justice through *hāpai*—a process of community accountability. A study by the New Zealand Ministry of Justice found that participants in Maori restorative circles reported higher satisfaction compared to those navigating traditional legal systems. Offenders were more likely to take responsibility, and victims felt heard and validated. It wasn't just about resolving incidents; it was about rebuilding trust and ensuring both parties could move forward without carrying the weight of unresolved hurt.

Modern research echoes these ancient truths. In schools across the United States, districts implementing restorative practices have seen suspensions drop by 30% and conflicts decrease by 25% (American Bar Association, 2016). Students participating in restorative circles were 35% more likely to say they felt treated fairly—proof that when justice is rooted in connection rather than punishment, everyone benefits. Even within the criminal justice system, restorative programs have led to a 14% reduction in repeat offenses, according to research by Sherman and Strang (2007).

But restorative practices aren't just about policy shifts or structured programs. At their core, they reflect a way of being—a mindset that prioritizes accountability and healing in every interaction. As Van Ness and Strong (2014) highlight, the true power of restoration lies in its ability to heal emotional wounds, foster empathy, and strengthen relationships. It's not just about resolving conflict but transforming how we engage with one another, both in moments of ease and moments of tension.

My Journey to Restorative Power

This understanding shifted everything for me. As I immersed myself in the restorative movement, both as a practitioner and educator, I realized that being restorative wasn't just about tools or frameworks used in professional settings. It had to be personal. It had to shape how I showed up in my family, friendships, and community. That's when I developed the concept I call *Restorative Power*.

Restorative Power goes beyond structured practices—it's an internal discipline, a daily commitment to lead with empathy, accountability, and courage in every relationship. It starts at home, in the conversations we avoid, the frustrations we suppress, and the boundaries we either ignore or enforce without compassion. I've seen its impact firsthand: in moments where I chose honest dialogue over silence, accountability over defensiveness, and reconciliation over avoidance.

This chapter explores what *Restorative Power* looks like in real life—how we can move from theory to practice, not just in schools, workplaces, or communities, but in the heart of our everyday relationships. This is because genuine restoration doesn't start with systems or policies. It begins with us.

Examples of Restorative Power

In my work as an educator, husband, and father, I've witnessed firsthand how restorative practices can transform relationships and environments:

As an Educator: Restorative practices have transformed my classroom into a space of trust and growth. I remember working with a student who had been labeled as "troubled" and "disruptive." Instead of isolating him, I invited him to share his story in a restorative circle. Through this process, he opened up about the challenges he was facing at home. This shift in dynamic allowed him to feel seen, valued, and connected to the classroom community. Over time, his behavior changed—not because of punishment, but because of the support and accountability that restorative practices provided.

As a Husband: In marriage, Restorative Power has taught me that love thrives in accountability. My wife and I have navigated difficult conversations where vulnerability and patience were the keys to resolution. For instance, during a particularly challenging season, we committed to weekly check-ins where we could share both frustrations and gratitude. These conversations required us to actively listen, set aside defensiveness, and commit to repairing misunderstandings rather than letting them fester.

As a Father: Being restorative as a parent means modeling accountability and empathy for my daughter. When I make mistakes—such as losing my temper—I own up to them and apologize. This helps repair the moment and teaches her the importance of taking responsibility for her actions. It shows her that making mistakes is part of being human, but what matters is how we repair the harm and move forward.

Relevance of Restorative Practices

Restorative practices are not just historical or theoretical; they are a timely and relevant response to the challenges we face in today's world. These practices offer a much-needed antidote in an age marked by division, isolation, and the rapid pace of life. Whether addressing systemic injustices, workplace conflicts, or interpersonal struggles, restorative practices remind us of our shared humanity and the power of healing over harm.

Consider the context of the global mental health crisis. People are more connected than ever digitally, yet feelings of loneliness and disconnection are on the rise. Restorative practices provide a way to rebuild those lost connections by creating spaces where individuals feel heard, valued, and supported. They are particularly crucial in schools, where children often face significant social and emotional challenges. By integrating restorative approaches, educators can help students develop emotional intelligence, resilience, and a sense of belonging.

What Are People Using Instead, and What Are the Results?

Despite their potential, restorative practices are not always the go-to approach. Many individuals and organizations still rely on punitive systems, zero-tolerance policies, or avoidance strategies. In schools, for example, suspensions and expulsions are still widely used as disciplinary measures. While these methods may remove a problem temporarily, they rarely address the underlying issues or teach students how to make better choices. Instead, they often lead to alienation, resentment, and higher dropout rates.

In personal relationships, avoidance and blame are common coping mechanisms. When conflicts arise, many people choose to withdraw or assign fault rather than engage in the vulnerable work of repair. Such behavior can lead to fractured relationships and unresolved tensions that resurface later. In workplaces, punitive responses to mistakes—such as public reprimands or dismissals—often create cultures of fear rather than growth. The results are clear: these approaches perpetuate harm, disconnection, and cycles of mistrust.

Challenges and Barriers to Implementation

While restorative practices hold great promise, they are not without challenges. Implementing them requires time, patience, and a willingness to embrace vulnerability. In many institutions, the fast pace and pressure for quick fixes make it difficult to invest in the deeper work of dialogue and repair. Additionally, cultural resistance and skepticism can arise, as restorative practices often challenge long-held beliefs about punishment and accountability.

One of the biggest barriers is the misconception that restorative practices are "soft" or lack consequences. In reality, these practices demand a high level of accountability and effort from everyone involved. They require individuals to confront the harm they've caused, take responsibility, and actively participate in repairing relationships. The process can be uncomfortable and challenging, especially in environments where punitive approaches have been the norm.

Another challenge is the need for proper training and resources. Facilitating restorative circles, for example, requires skill, preparation, and an understanding of group dynamics. Without these, attempts at implementation can fall short, leading to frustration or skepticism about the approach.

The Cost of Not Embracing Restorative Power

The inability to develop and embody Restorative Power has cost us dearly. It cost my father his life, just as it's killing men silently, day after day. My father was a good man, but he struggled to create the healing spaces within himself that he so desperately needed. He was like so many men around us—strong and striving, but often carrying his pain alone. When we don't build the skill to restore our hearts, we become isolated. We lose the chance to heal, and we leave wounds that fester inside and around us. For men especially, these wounds stay hidden under layers of strength and self-sufficiency. But left unchecked, they claim lives.

Restorative Power is a practice designed not just for one setting but as a foundation for a life built on connection, healing, and integrity. It's about embodying a way of being that can breathe life into our relationships, our communities, and our work. Through this journey, I invite you to explore how this power can transform not just our external relationships but also our inner lives, in ways that can truly heal and restore.

Action Steps

1. Think about a recent conflict in your life. What would have been different if you had approached it with a restorative mindset, focusing on understanding and repairing rather than reacting?
2. Reflect on the relationships in your life where trust and open communication are strong. What habits or practices contribute to those bonds? How might you apply

similar practices to relationships that need healing or strengthening?

3. How do you currently respond to situations where others' actions go against your values? What steps could you take to align your reactions more closely with a restorative approach, creating an opportunity for growth and mutual respect?

CHAPTER FOUR

The Power of Alignment

Growing up, I witnessed a relentless disconnect between people's dreams and the way they lived. Work took its toll, relationships felt draining, and everyone seemed trapped in a cycle of adjusting to circumstances that didn't align with their true desires. This misalignment bred exhaustion, frustration, and a perpetual chase for an elusive sense of fulfillment.

I saw this pattern in my family, my community, and my surroundings. People worked tirelessly, endured relationships that sapped their energy, and held onto the hope that things would somehow improve. Watching these struggles planted a seed in me—a determination to live differently. I wanted a life where my values, relationships, and ambitions were in harmony—a life where everything I invested in resonated deeply with who I am.

My Journey to Alignment

Building alignment in my life has been an intentional and continuous process. For me, alignment is about knowing who I am and making choices that honor that identity in every role I hold. It's about saying yes to the things that bring me closer to my mission and no to the things that don't. This commitment to alignment has shaped every aspect of my life—from my family and career to my friendships.

One of the most significant ways I've created alignment is through the relationship I've built with my wife, Melissa. Marrying her was a decision deeply rooted in alignment. She's my best friend, my partner, and my dream girl. Melissa embodies qualities I admire—strength, compassion, and wisdom—and our relationship reflects my values of love, growth, and joy. She inspires me, grounds me, and challenges me to be better in every way.

Our partnership is not something I need to manage or compromise on—it's an anchor. It enhances my ability to be a better man, father, friend, and husband. Melissa represents the intentionality behind my pursuit of alignment, and she reflects what happens when our choices resonate with who we are at our core.

It is because of her that I feel deeply indebted to reciprocate my love for her through protection, care, support, and peace. I recognize the gift she is in my life, and I am committed to ensuring that she feels seen, cherished, and valued every day. Our bond goes beyond the surface—it's a sacred connection built on trust, respect, and mutual growth. I will work for as long as we are together to pursue getting better as individuals and as partners each day. This commitment isn't just for today or tomorrow—it's a lifelong promise to continue evolving together, growing stronger, and lifting each other up. With Melissa by my side, I know that together, we will navigate the journey of life in a way that reflects the deepest alignment of our hearts and values.

This same pursuit extends to my work. I have committed myself to a career that aligns with my values and purpose. My mission is to help people find the power in their vulnerability and use it as a tool for success and fulfillment. Vulnerability is not a weakness—it is strength, and I am passionate about helping others unlock this power. Whether I'm coaching, speaking, or developing curriculum, my work is a natural extension of who I am. It allows me to live in alignment with my values every day.

The Science Behind Alignment

Alignment isn't just a personal philosophy—it's backed by research. Dr. Rangan Chatterjee explains that alignment between our inner values and external actions is the key to living a fulfilled and purposeful life. When we live in alignment, we experience less stress, greater focus, and deeper satisfaction. Misalignment, on the other hand, can lead to exhaustion and disengagement.

Consider this: Have you ever been on a team where everyone seemed to have a different agenda? Or have you ever felt that something you were doing required far more effort than it should? These situations often stem from misalignment. When our values and actions are disconnected, we feel a sense of resistance and burnout.

Research also shows that alignment increases efficiency and collaboration. In corporate settings, when team members' personal values align with the organization's mission, engagement soars. A cohesive team moving in the same direction creates a compounding effect—energy builds on energy, leading to greater success.

Lessons in Alignment from Others

Some of the most successful organizations in the world thrive because they prioritize alignment between their core values and daily operations.

Take Chick-fil-A, for example. Beyond selling chicken sandwiches, Chick-fil-A is deeply rooted in its core values of hospitality, excellence, and care. From its signature "my pleasure" response to its commitment to closing on Sundays to honor family and faith, everything about the company is aligned with what it stands for. Employees understand the culture and expectations, which makes the customer experience consistent and memorable.

Similarly, SoulCycle has built a community around its values of inspiration, movement, and connection. It's more than just a spin class—it's an experience that fosters personal transformation. Instructors, music choices, and even the design of the studios all contribute to a culture that aligns with its mission. This type of atmosphere is why people aren't just attending workouts; they're becoming part of something bigger.

These organizations understand that alignment isn't just a philosophy—it's a business strategy. When employees and customers resonate with a company's values, loyalty deepens, performance improves, and the overall mission is strengthened.

Challenges and Triumphs in Alignment

Alignment isn't always easy to achieve. I've faced my share of challenges along the way. Early in my marriage, Melissa and I had to navigate differing perspectives and priorities. Creating alignment required honest conversations, compromise, and a commitment to grow together. It wasn't always comfortable, but it was worth it.

Similarly, in my work, I've faced moments where I had to choose between opportunities that seemed promising and those that truly aligned with my mission. Saying no to lucrative offers or high-profile projects isn't easy, but staying true to my values has always brought long-term rewards.

These challenges taught me that alignment is not a one-time achievement—it's a continual process of reflection and adjustment. It requires courage, clarity, and a willingness to prioritize what matters most.

Building Alignment in Your Life

So, how can you build alignment in your own life? Start by reflecting on what truly matters to you. What are your core values? What brings you joy and fulfillment? Once you've identified these, use them as a guide to evaluate your choices and relationships.

When organizations like Chick-fil-A and SoulCycle maintain strong cultures of alignment, they don't do it by accident—they do it through clear values, intentional decision-making, and a commitment to what they stand for. The same is true for your personal life.

If you want alignment, you have to be intentional. Define your values, set boundaries, and say no to things that pull you away from your mission. Whether it's your career, your relationships, or your personal growth, every decision should be a step toward a life that feels whole and fulfilling.

Two Entrepreneurs: Stories of Alignment and Misalignment

Story 1: The Aligned Entrepreneur

Jasmine had always been a visionary entrepreneur. She dreamed of building a business that not only provided for her family but also aligned with her core values of integrity, creativity, and community. However, she realized that success would mean little if it didn't reflect who she truly was.

One morning, Jasmine sat down with a notebook and defined her core values. She chose integrity, creativity, and community as the principles that would guide her decisions. Writing them down gave her clarity and focus. She began revisiting them weekly, using them as her compass whenever new opportunities arose.

Next, Jasmine visualized her ideal life. She pictured herself working on projects that fueled her creativity while being present for her family and actively contributing to her community. This vision felt authentic and deeply fulfilling, and it became her north star.

When she evaluated her current situation, Jasmine noticed some misalignments. Her workload left little room for family time, and her client base didn't align with her values of integrity and community. She made tough decisions to drop clients who didn't align and scaled back on commitments that drained her energy.

She then crafted a mission statement: "To inspire and uplift others through creative, community-focused solutions." This mission became her guiding principle as she built her business.

Jasmine also learned to set boundaries. She began saying no to projects that didn't align with her mission, even if they were financially appealing. These changes gave her more time and energy to focus on what mattered most.

Taking small steps, Jasmine restructured her schedule to include weekly family nights and partnered with local organizations to create community-driven initiatives. She didn't overhaul her life overnight but made intentional changes over time.

Every month, Jasmine reflected on her progress. She journaled about how her life and work aligned with her values, and when she noticed areas that needed improvement, she adjusted accordingly.

One evening, as Jasmine wrapped up a community workshop, she paused to celebrate. She had created a thriving business that resonated with her values and supported her ideal life. She realized that each step toward alignment was a victory, and she was living proof of what's possible when you prioritize what truly matters.

Story 2: The Misaligned Entrepreneur

Derek had big dreams. His startup was growing rapidly, and he was working tirelessly to keep up. On paper, he was successful. But deep down, Derek felt drained, disconnected, and uncertain about his path.

Derek had never taken the time to define his core values. Instead, he chased whatever seemed profitable or urgent. His days were a whirlwind of back-to-back meetings, endless emails, and decisions made on the fly. Without a compass to guide him, he often said yes to projects that left him feeling empty.

NO MORE DANCING

He rarely paused to visualize his ideal life. If he had, he might have seen a version of himself spending more time with his family and less time tethered to his phone. He might have imagined a business that made a positive impact on the world instead of one that simply chased revenue.

One night, after another 14-hour workday, Derek evaluated his situation. His relationships were strained, his health was deteriorating, and his work felt misaligned with his deeper sense of purpose. But instead of making adjustments, he convinced himself to push through, hoping things would improve on their own.

Without a mission statement, Derek lacked a clear sense of purpose. He often felt pulled in multiple directions, unsure of which opportunities to pursue. Saying no was nearly impossible for him, and he found himself overwhelmed by commitments that didn't serve him.

Derek's lack of boundaries took a toll. He constantly sacrificed his time, energy, and focus for others, leaving little for himself. His personal life suffered, and his business began to lose the innovative edge that had set it apart.

Months passed, and Derek felt stuck in the same cycle. He never took small steps to improve his situation, telling himself he didn't have the time. Reflection wasn't part of his routine, so he never assessed where adjustments were needed.

The breaking point came when a key team member resigned, citing burnout and a lack of direction. Derek realized that his lack of alignment wasn't just affecting him—it was impacting his entire team.

Looking back, Derek regretted not celebrating the small wins along the way. He was so focused on the big picture that he overlooked the progress he had made. His journey felt like an endless grind instead of a series of meaningful milestones.

Feeling the weight of misalignment, Derek finally decided to make a change. Though it was late in the game, he resolved to revisit his values, visualize his ideal life, and take small steps toward align It was a tough road, but he learned that it's never too late to course-correct and build a life that reflects who you truly are.

The Fulfillment of Alignment

The beauty of alignment is that it creates a life of harmony and purpose. My family, work, and community all reinforce each other, creating a unified vision of who I am and who I want to become. I'm not pulled in conflicting directions; instead, every choice I make strengthens the others.

Alignment isn't something you find by accident—it's something you build intentionally. It's a commitment to live authentically, to choose relationships and work that resonate with your heart, and to let go of anything that doesn't. The journey to alignment may not always be easy, but the fulfillment it brings is worth every ounce of effort.

So I ask you, what's your focus? What drives you, brings you joy, and reflects your values? And how can you begin building alignment in your life today?

The power of alignment is transformative. It's the key to living a life of purpose, passion, and fulfillment. By aligning your values, actions, and relationships, you can create a life that feels not only successful but truly meaningful. The journey begins with a single step—start building your alignment today.

CHAPTER FIVE

The F Word

Let's talk about the "F" word. Not the one that first comes to mind, but a different one: Fear. The fear of addressing conflict, the fear of standing our ground, the fear of saying what needs to be said. Fear often masquerades in corporate settings or communities as disengagement. It creates psychological barriers that inhibit risk-taking, creativity, and growth. In these environments, the absence of psychological safety—the belief that one can speak up without negative consequences—only compounds these challenges.

This chapter is about learning to push through fear and speak up, even when it feels risky. It's about the power of boundaries, the clarity they provide, and the freedom that comes from saying what you mean.

Framing Fear in Corporate and Personal Contexts

Fear in a corporate setting is often unspoken but visible. It's the hesitancy in meetings, the reluctance to share new ideas, or the unwillingness to give feedback. This disengagement costs teams their edge and fosters a culture of "playing it safe." However, when a leader creates a safe space—one where employees feel empowered to take risks—the possibilities for growth multiply.

Take one of the well-known leaders in NFL history, a quote from football player Ray Lewis, for example: "It is better to be respected than liked." In the workplace, likability can feel safer, but respect drives results. High performers like Michael Jordan and Kobe Bryant exemplify this principle. They weren't necessarily liked all the time, but they earned respect because they demanded the best from themselves and others. Respect, paired with psychological safety, is the foundation for building high-functioning teams.

The Power of Boundaries: Melissa's Story

There's one moment that stands out for me, a moment that changed the way I saw both boundaries and my wife, Melissa. We were just friends back then, joking around like we often did. Somewhere in the laughter, I let slip a casual, joking "F*** you." Melissa stopped mid-laugh, looked me dead in the eyes, and said, "Don't ever curse at me again. Whether we're joking or not, that kind of language leads to a habit of cursing at each other. If we do it when things are good, we'll end up doing it when things are bad. I don't want that kind of friendship or relationship."

Her delivery was calm but firm. She didn't explain herself unnecessarily, nor did she linger on the moment. She just switched topics and kept the conversation going.

At that moment, I felt both a sting and a shift. I realized that her boundary wasn't about control; it was about creating a safe, respectful dynamic. And instead of diminishing my view of her, it made me respect her even more. From that day forward, I never cursed at her again—not once in the next eight years.

Melissa's courage taught me an important lesson: boundaries aren't walls meant to keep people out; they're markers that define how we engage with one another.

Boundaries in Leadership

Boundaries in leadership function much like the rules of a basketball game. Imagine playing a game with no out-of-bounds lines. At first, it might seem liberating, but soon, the chaos would make the game unplayable. Boundaries, like those lines, don't restrict us—they enhance the experience by providing structure, clarity, and trust.

In relationships and organizations, a lack of boundaries leads to collateral damage: disorganization, reduced engagement, and resentment. Leaders who avoid setting boundaries may seem accommodating at first but often fail to build the trust and respect necessary for long-term success.

Companies that prioritize clear communication and strong boundaries tend to outperform those that steer clear of difficult conversations. For example, Netflix's high-performance culture is built on radical candor and accountability. Employees know where they stand, which fosters both respect and innovation.

Fear vs. Growth

Growth requires stepping into discomfort, a fact that both Michael Jordan and Kobe Bryant understood. These athletes didn't push boundaries to be liked—they did it to achieve greatness. However, as leaders, they had to balance their intensity with respect for their teams. While pushing too hard can alienate others, avoiding confrontation altogether stifles growth.

The same principle applies to everyday life. Fear tells us to avoid conflict, but avoiding it only strengthens its grip. Addressing fear head-on—whether through confrontation, setting boundaries, or embracing vulnerability—is the key to unlocking potential.

Cultural Consistency and the Impact of Small Habits

One of the most profound lessons Melissa taught me was about the power of consistency. Her stance on not cursing wasn't just about language—it was about creating a culture of respect.

Habits formed in good times carry into bad times. If we're careless when life is easy, that carelessness will amplify during challenges.

Consistency builds trust, both in ourselves and in others. It's what separates leaders who inspire from those who merely manage. Culture isn't defined by grand gestures but by the small, consistent actions we take every day.

NO MORE DANCING

Teaching Confrontation: The Ripple Effect

Melissa's example of confronting me wasn't just about setting a boundary; it was a masterclass in conflict resolution. By addressing the issue calmly and moving on, she showed that confrontation doesn't have to lead to conflict. Instead, it can be a moment of clarity and growth.

Imagine if leaders approached feedback this way—addressing issues with respect, clarity, and confidence, then moving forward without holding a grudge. It's a simple yet powerful approach that fosters trust and accountability.

Here are two stories of someone in a healthy work relationship and someone in an unhealthy work relationship, showing the impact of applying or neglecting the action steps for standing your ground:

Story 1: The Healthy Work Relationship

Maria had always been passionate about her work, but she realized she was struggling to maintain her sense of self in the workplace. She made the decision to assert herself and set healthier boundaries with her colleagues.

Maria began by identifying her boundaries. She reflected on moments where she felt uncomfortable or disrespected, like when coworkers interrupted her during meetings or expected her to answer emails late at night. She wrote down her boundaries: uninterrupted speaking time, a no-work-after-hours policy, and clear expectations for collaboration.

To prepare herself, Maria practiced setting boundaries. She role-played with a friend, saying things like, "I feel more effective when I'm able to finish my thoughts without interruption" or "I've set a rule for myself to disconnect from work after 6 PM to recharge." Using "I" statements helped her express her needs without sounding accusatory.

Maria started small. The next time a coworker interrupted her in a meeting, she politely but firmly said, "I'd like to finish my point before we move on." Though her heart raced, the positive response she received boosted her confidence.

Setting boundaries wasn't always comfortable, but Maria embraced the discomfort. She reminded herself that each boundary she set was a step toward respecting herself and teaching others to respect her too.

She remained consistent. When a team member emailed her late at night, Maria didn't respond until the next morning. Over time, her colleagues began to respect her boundaries, and Maria noticed a positive shift in her work relationships.

Every time Maria successfully set a boundary, she celebrated. Whether it was treating herself to her favorite coffee or simply acknowledging her progress in her journal, these small rewards kept her motivated.

As a result, Maria's work relationships flourished. Her colleagues admired her clarity and confidence, and she felt more empowered and fulfilled in her role. Standing her ground transformed her work environment into a space where she could thrive.

NO MORE DANCING

Story 2: The Unhealthy Work Relationship

James loved his job, but over time, he started feeling drained and unappreciated. He often stayed late, answered emails at all hours, and tolerated dismissive comments from his manager. Deep down, James knew things needed to change, but he didn't know where to start.

James hadn't identified his boundaries. He felt uncomfortable when his manager criticized him in front of others or when coworkers handed off last-minute tasks, but he brushed these feelings aside, unsure how to address them. Without clarity on what behaviors crossed the line, James felt stuck.

When he tried to speak up, James avoided direct communication. Instead of saying, "I feel disrespected when I'm criticized publicly," he stayed silent or vented to friends outside of work. His fear of confrontation kept him from practicing boundary-setting in a constructive way.

James also struggled to start small. He waited for big blowups to try to address issues, which often led to emotionally charged conversations that didn't resolve anything. This pattern left him feeling even more defeated.

The discomfort of setting boundaries overwhelmed James. Whenever he considered standing up for himself, he worried about retaliation or being seen as difficult. To avoid conflict, he continued to tolerate behaviors that made him unhappy.

Inconsistency compounded the problem. On rare occasions, James pushed back against unreasonable demands, but he would quickly cave under pressure. This made it hard for others to take his boundaries seriously.

James rarely celebrated his small wins because he didn't see them as victories. Instead, he focused on the negative, reinforcing his belief that his efforts were futile.

Over time, the lack of boundaries took its toll. James felt burned out, undervalued, and resentful. His relationships with coworkers and his manager became strained, and he began to question whether he belonged in the company at all.

Reflecting on his experience, James realized he needed to make a change. He committed to identifying his boundaries, practicing small steps, and embracing the discomfort of standing up for himself. While it was a difficult journey, James learned that building healthy work relationships required intentional effort and self-respect.

Fear will always be present, but it doesn't have to control you. When you set boundaries, you reclaim your power and create a foundation of trust and respect. Whether in your personal relationships or professional life, the courage to confront fear is what separates mediocrity from greatness.

Fear and Boundaries: The Invisible Connection

Fear and boundaries are deeply connected, often in ways we don't initially recognize. At its core, fear thrives in uncertainty—the fear of disappointing others, the fear of rejection, or the fear of being seen as difficult. These anxieties make it challenging to establish and maintain boundaries, even when we know they're necessary.

The hesitation to set boundaries is often rooted in the fear of conflict or the potential fallout of standing firm. Many people worry that if they enforce their limits, they'll be labeled as uncooperative, selfish, or too rigid. But in reality, failing to set boundaries creates a different kind of problem—one where resentment builds, self-respect erodes, and relationships (both personal and professional) suffer.

Boundaries are a direct response to fear. They are the tools we use to define what is and isn't acceptable, ensuring that fear doesn't dictate our decisions. The moment we recognize our own discomfort and act on it by setting a boundary, we reclaim control over our environment and interactions.

Consider a workplace scenario: An employee consistently takes on extra responsibilities out of fear that saying "no" will make them seem less dedicated. Over time, this person becomes overwhelmed, exhausted, and disengaged. But what if they had set a clear boundary from the start? By expressing their capacity and limits, they wouldn't just protect their own well-being—they would also foster respect from colleagues who understand their expectations.

The same applies to personal relationships. When Melissa set her boundary with me about cursing, she wasn't acting out of fear—she was acting out of self-respect. But what if she had been too afraid to say anything? What if she had let it slide, uncomfortable but silent? Over time, that discomfort would have turned into frustration, potentially damaging our friendship before it even had the chance to grow.

Fear tells us to avoid boundaries because they might create conflict. But the truth is, avoiding boundaries only leads to deeper conflict—internally and externally. The more we practice setting and maintaining boundaries, the more we condition ourselves to move through fear rather than be controlled by it.

The lesson is clear: Fear loses its power when we choose to stand our ground. Boundaries aren't just about protecting ourselves; they're about creating clarity, trust, and healthy dynamics. They ensure that fear doesn't hold the pen when writing the story of our lives.

CHAPTER SIX

Building Community

In the summer of 2018, my journey in restorative practices took a transformative turn. Mohamad Maarouf, then director of KIPP Houston High School, reached out with an opportunity to take on a pioneering role as the school's first Restorative Justice Coordinator. The goal? To shift the school culture from punitive approaches to one built on restoration and understanding. My role was multifaceted: support teachers and administrators in managing student behaviors, develop a restorative discipline plan, and teach a course called Honor Council.

I didn't want just any council class. I had two requests. First, I wanted to rename the course to the Restorative Power (RP) Council, and second, I wanted to empower the students in this course to become Restorative Power Coordinator Assistants, taking active roles as peer mediators and support figures.

The name "Restorative Power Council" was inspired by my belief in giving students the tools to take back their power and own the skills of a restorative lifestyle. I envisioned a space where they wouldn't just learn about conflict resolution but would actively embody it, taking charge of their personal growth and community impact. I wanted the name to reflect a sense of agency and transformation—a council where students weren't passive participants but powerful agents of change within their school environment.

And so, the RP Council was born, marking the beginning of an unforgettable journey in community-building.

Understanding the Pressures of KIPP Students

Very quickly, I realized that the students at KIPP bore immense pressures. They were balancing the rigorous academic standards KIPP demanded with challenging responsibilities outside the classroom—some worked part-time to support their families, others acted as translators, and many took on responsibilities that extended far beyond their years. Many were striving to be the first in their families to attend college, carrying the weight of family expectations on their shoulders.

The silent suffering and struggles of these students were often invisible, yet the strain was undeniable. I knew that if we wanted to transform the school's culture, we had to create a place where students felt genuinely seen and supported.

Breaking Down the Walls

The first challenge was to break down the walls that students had built around themselves—walls of self-protection, stress, and silent endurance. I wanted the RP Council to be a space where students could shed those walls and connect.

We began with storytelling sessions, where students shared their personal journeys—their challenges, dreams, and fears. With each story, empathy grew within the room, and a foundation of trust began to take root.

In these sessions, students learned to communicate openly, listen deeply, and lead with compassion. As they connected, they realized they weren't alone in their struggles. This mutual understanding became the backbone of our community. Developing empathy helped them bond, and these connections went beyond the classroom, influencing interactions throughout the school.

Empowering the RP Council Members

With empathy as our foundation, I moved forward with training the RP Council students to become Restorative Justice Coordinator Assistants. This wasn't a simple task. Many of these students had never seen themselves as leaders, yet here they were, stepping up to help build a healthier school community.

We trained on active listening, conflict resolution, facilitating restorative circles, and even managing personal emotions in high-stress situations. The students practiced role-playing real scenarios they might encounter on campus. Their goal was to step in when conflicts arose and guide their peers toward understanding, not punishment. They were learning to support others, reflect on their behaviors, and strengthen the RP Council's culture of empathy and accountability.

Bringing the Work to Campus

Armed with training, the RP Council students began to put their skills to work on campus. Known across the school as leaders, they became the go-to figures for mediation, support, and understanding. They helped transform potential conflicts into growth opportunities, often de-escalating situations before they became disciplinary issues.

Over time, students and teachers began to see the impact of this approach: detentions and suspensions decreased, replaced by conversations and solutions rooted in empathy.

For many, the RP Council became a lifeline—a place to process experiences, voice challenges, and build a sense of genuine community. The council wasn't just a course; it became a movement within KIPP, a living testament to the power of restorative practices.

Seeking Support from All Levels

As effective as the RP Council was, we couldn't do it alone. Building a restorative community required collaboration. Teachers, administrators, and staff were invited into our restorative circles to learn alongside students. We worked together to integrate restorative practices across the school. With Mohammad Maarouf's unwavering support, we were able to foster a restorative culture that spread through the entire community, reinforcing our foundation.

Through this collaboration, we built a stronger, more resilient community—one that saw behavior as an opportunity for understanding, not a problem to be punished. Together, we created lasting change that could support both students and staff.

A Broader Mission and Personal Dedication

The RP Council was a turning point that inspired me to take this approach beyond KIPP. I wanted to share the power of restorative practices with other schools, both nationally and internationally. Through this experience, I recognized the impact of a well-designed, empathy-rooted curriculum. My mission became clear: to bring empathy, accountability, and support into classrooms everywhere.

But my journey had a deeper, personal drive. After my father's passing in 2019, I felt a profound shift in my purpose. My father, like so many others, longed for a community he could depend on—a place of acceptance and understanding. Yet he struggled to find and maintain such a space, and the isolation weighed on him. The loss pushed me to create communities that he needed but couldn't access, spaces where people feel valued, supported, and empowered.

In his memory, I expanded the RP Council into a comprehensive curriculum, one that schools across the globe could use. Each step I took was in honor of his life, building the kinds of communities he needed, helping others feel connected and seen. Today, I am committed to helping schools and organizations create supportive environments that nurture human connection.

CARLOS J. MALAVE

The Power of Community

Reflecting on the RP Council's impact, I am reminded of the immense power of a true community. When students feel part of something bigger, they face challenges with resilience, grow through adversity, and invest in each other's success.

Community-building is not just a methodology—it's a mindset, a belief in the potential of others, and a commitment to understanding. It's about breaking down walls and creating a space where individuals can rise above their struggles together.

The RP Council was proof of the transformative impact a supportive community can have. In building this foundation, we created a space for resilience, empathy, and growth—for everyone involved.

Here are two stories that highlight the transformative power of building a restorative community. The first tells the journey of Samantha, a student who thrived in an environment that embraced empathy, connection, and shared responsibility. The second follows Michael, whose school neglected these principles, leading to disconnection and missed opportunities. These stories show the stark contrast between the positive outcomes of prioritizing restorative practices and the challenges that arise when they are overlooked.

Story 1: Building a Healthy Community (Individual and Organizational Growth)

Samantha, a high school junior, had always struggled with expressing herself. She often felt misunderstood and isolated, leading to conflicts with her peers. Meanwhile, her school, Greenwood High, faced challenges with maintaining a sense of unity among students and staff. Determined to address these issues, the principal introduced a Restorative Justice (RJ) Council, applying the action steps for building community at both individual and organizational levels.

At first, Samantha participated in a one-on-one session with her RJ mentor, who helped her identify personal triggers and reflect on the pressures she faced. She realized her frustration stemmed from a fear of rejection. Inspired, she joined storytelling sessions where students shared their challenges and dreams. For the first time, Samantha felt seen and heard.

As her confidence grew, Samantha embraced empathy-building activities, learning to listen without judgment. She became a peer mediator, guiding others through conflicts using the restorative skills she had practiced in role-playing exercises. Seeing the positive impact, her teachers incorporated restorative practices into their classrooms, modeling active listening and conflict resolution. The entire school began to shift, with students and staff fostering deeper connections and shared purpose.

By the end of the year, Samantha was not just thriving individually but was part of a community that valued empathy and accountability. Greenwood High even documented its success, creating workshops for other schools to replicate their restorative framework. Samantha proudly represented her school in these workshops, inspiring others to embrace a culture of restoration.

Story 2: The Consequences of Ignoring Community-Building

At Riverbend Academy, the absence of restorative practices led to growing tension among students and staff. Michael, a senior, often lashed out in class, earning the label of a "troublemaker." Unaddressed systemic issues created a lack of trust between students and teachers. The administration saw these problems but dismissed the importance of addressing them through community-building.

Michael's teachers didn't take time to understand his personal challenges or stressors. Storytelling and empathy-building sessions were nonexistent, leaving Michael to internalize his struggles. His peers saw him as confrontational, but no one took the time to dig deeper. Without a safe space for connection, Michael's behavior escalated. He was suspended multiple times, each punishment alienating him further.

The ripple effect extended beyond Michael. Teachers became increasingly frustrated with their inability to connect with students, leading to a rigid, punitive school environment. There was no focus on training educators in restorative practices or creating a shared sense of purpose. The result? A fractured community where mistrust and disengagement thrived.

By the time Michael graduated, he left Riverbend feeling unsupported and disconnected. The school had missed the opportunity to empower him and other students as leaders. Worse, Riverbend's culture continued to deteriorate, with rising disciplinary issues and declining morale among staff. Unlike Greenwood High, Riverbend lacked the framework to reflect on its failures and create meaningful change.

Conclusion: Embracing the Power of Community

The stories of Samantha and Michael highlight the profound impact that community-building, rooted in restorative practices, can have on both individuals and organizations. When we make the effort to build inclusive, empathetic communities, we create spaces where individuals can thrive, learn, and grow. Through empathy, understanding, and shared responsibility, we transform lives and shape the future of the communities we nurture.

As educators, leaders, and members of society, we have a choice: to embrace the transformative power of restorative practices or to allow isolation, mistrust, and disengagement to thrive. It is in our hands to foster environments where people—especially our young people—feel seen, supported, and valued. These are the spaces where true growth happens, where individuals are empowered to become leaders and agents of change.

Building community is not a one-time effort; it is an ongoing commitment to creating connection, healing, and resilience. It requires continuous dedication, patience, and openness to learning from each other. But when we rise to this challenge, we create something far greater than a school, an organization, or a team—we create a culture of belonging, where everyone has the opportunity to reach their fullest potential.

Let us commit to this journey of building community, not just within our schools but in every aspect of our lives. Through restorative practices, we can change the narrative, one person at a time, one community at a time, and ultimately, we can build a world where empathy, accountability, and connection reign. The challenge is great, but the reward is immeasurable. Together, we can create a legacy of compassion, growth, and transformation for generations to come.

CHAPTER SEVEN

Legacy

Legacy is a word that often brings to mind grand accomplishments, but for me, legacy is more personal than that. It's not about titles, accolades, or public recognition. Legacy, at its core, is about the memories we leave with the people who matter most. It's about the moments that become etched in the hearts of those we love—moments that last far beyond our physical presence.

The Personal Side of Legacy

My father taught me this lesson in a profound way. Growing up, he made sure that my siblings and I had countless memories to hold onto. He created spaces for us to come together, not through grand gestures but simple, everyday acts. Movie nights were his favorite. Even when we resisted, he'd insist on rallying everyone into the same room to laugh, debate, or share tears over something silly or serious. These nights were his way of weaving himself into our lives, making sure he'd always be there in the moments we'd later recall with fondness.

On the basketball court, my father didn't hold back. It wasn't just a game; it was his way of teaching us resilience, teamwork, and connection. We laughed, joked, and sometimes fought, but those moments became the foundation of love and connection that stayed with me forever. Even now, I carry the lessons learned during those "little" moments.

After my father passed, my wife shaped my understanding of legacy further. While grieving his death, I resisted her idea of erasing our debt as a step toward creating a different kind of legacy. She reminded me that legacy isn't just about memories but also about the freedom to take risks and shape the future for ourselves and our family. Together, we became debt-free, and our daughter, Thais, witnessed the sacrifices and rewards firsthand. That experience became part of our family legacy—modeling resilience, teamwork, and vision for her future.

Legacy in Leadership: A Corporate Lens

Legacy isn't just personal—it extends to organizations, communities, and leaders. Corporations, like individuals, leave legacies that outlast them. The question is, what kind of legacy are they leaving? Are they focused solely on resume-like accomplishments, such as profits and accolades, or are they shaping a future through the small, everyday moments that truly matter?

Consider the contrast between an obituary and a resume. A resume lists achievements, titles, and measurable results, but an obituary tells the story of impact—who showed up for you and why. Similarly, a corporate legacy isn't just about stock prices or awards; it's about how employees feel, the culture that's cultivated, and the meaningful moments that ripple outward.

Organizations, like my father, can create small yet significant moments for their employees. A simple acknowledgment of effort, celebrating milestones, or fostering spaces for authentic connection is one of the "little" moments that make a workplace more human. Much like the memories my father created for me, these moments in the workplace are not little at all—they become the foundation of a company's lasting impact.

Little Moments: Shaping the Future

My father's intentionality in creating memories taught me a profound truth: the little moments aren't little at all. They are the ones we remember most, the ones that shape who we are. In the same way, leaders and organizations shape their legacies through seemingly small actions.

Think about schools: a teacher who takes a moment to encourage a struggling student might change the trajectory of that student's life. In corporations, a manager who takes time to recognize an employee's contributions creates loyalty, inspiration, and motivation. These moments add up to a culture, a legacy of care, and a future where people feel seen and valued.

My father's basketball games with us weren't just games—they were monumental acts of connection. In schools and corporations, these "little" moments are the equivalent of shared spaces where people can thrive. Legacy, whether personal or corporate, is built in these moments.

Legacy in Culture: Standing on Change

Individuals who defy expectations create some of the most impactful legacies. Celebrities like Magic Johnson, Ava DuVernay, and Nipsey Hussle offer powerful examples. Magic Johnson didn't just build businesses—he created opportunities and revitalized communities, leaving a legacy of empowerment. Ava DuVernay told stories that needed to be heard, amplifying underrepresented voices and opening doors for others in Hollywood. Nipsey Hussle built a legacy of ownership and entrepreneurship, showing his community that they could invest in themselves and create generational wealth.

These individuals didn't dance around the hard issues—they confronted them head-on, standing for something larger than themselves. Their legacies aren't just about fame; they are about impact, change, and creating opportunities for others.

Dancing Around Legacy

Too often, legacy is stunted by a tendency to "dance around" issues. Instead of addressing what truly matters, we focus on surface-level accomplishments, avoiding the deeper, harder work of creating lasting impact. Organizations may prioritize optics over substance, individuals may prioritize appearances over authenticity, and leaders may avoid the tough conversations necessary for real change.

But legacy isn't built on avoidance. It's built on intention, courage, and the willingness to address the issues that matter most. This is why I titled this book "No More Dancing." It's a call to action to stop avoiding the hard work of legacy-building and start leaning into the moments that truly matter.

Conclusion: What's Being Left?

At the end of the day, legacy is about what we leave behind—not just in achievements but in the lives we've touched and the futures we've shaped. For me, it's the memories I create with my daughter, the lessons I learned from my father, and the freedom my wife and I built together. For organizations, it's the culture they create, the care they give their employees, and their community impact.

Legacy is deeply personal, but it's also universal. It's built in the little moments that add up to something far greater. Whether in our families, our schools, or our workplaces, we have the power to shape a legacy of connection, care, and impact—if we stop dancing around the issues and step into the work that truly matters.

Here's a story about a father's journey to building a legacy of connection:

David had always dreamed of leaving more than material wealth for his children—he wanted to leave a legacy of love, connection, and cherished memories. As a single father of two, Emma and Jordan, he realized that the moments they shared would shape the foundation of their family's identity for generations to come.

Step 1: Creating Intentional Rituals

David decided to establish family movie nights every Friday. They'd rotate who picked the film and always end the evening discussing their favorite scenes over homemade popcorn. Beyond the movies, David introduced weekend bike rides—a shared passion they discovered during a local charity event. Every Saturday morning, the trio would explore new trails, laughing, racing, and stopping for picnics. These rituals became their anchor, even during the busiest weeks.

Step 2: Building One-on-One Time

David wanted his children to feel seen as individuals. On Wednesday evenings, he'd take Emma to her favorite bookstore, where they'd browse shelves and chat over hot cocoa. Thursdays were reserved for Jordan, who loved basketball. They'd shoot hoops at the park, talking about school, friends, and dreams. During these moments, David practiced active listening, letting his children know their thoughts and feelings mattered deeply to him.

Step 3: Sharing Stories of Family Tradition

David began telling Emma and Jordan stories about their grandparents—how their grandmother loved to bake pies and how their grandfather taught him to fish. He shared lessons he had learned growing up, weaving humor and wisdom into every tale. One evening, he spoke about the meaning of legacy, explaining why creating memories and sharing values mattered. "It's not just about us," he told them. "It's about what we pass on to the next generation."

Step 4: Prioritizing Unplugged Quality Time

To ensure their time together was meaningful, David established "no-tech zones" during family activities. Phones and devices were left in a basket by the door, and they focused solely on each other. During family dinners, he encouraged open conversations, asking about their highs and lows of the day. Emma shared her dreams of becoming a writer, and Jordan revealed his love for art—passions David wouldn't have uncovered without these moments.

Step 5: Capturing and Documenting Memories

David began documenting their adventures. He took photos of their bike rides, family dinners, and even quiet moments reading on the couch. Together, they created a scrapbook, with each person contributing captions or drawings. The book became a tangible reflection of their journey—a keepsake they revisited on rainy days, laughing and reminiscing.

Step 6: Celebrating Milestones and Little Wins

David made it a point to celebrate achievements, big or small. When Emma finished her first short story, they held a "publishing party" with cupcakes and readings. When Jordan aced his art project, David displayed it proudly in their living room. These celebrations reminded the children that their efforts were seen and valued.

Step 7: Being the Example

David lived the values he wanted to instill. He showed kindness to strangers, resilience during tough times, and empathy toward others. He encouraged Emma and Jordan to explore how they could impact the world. "What kind of legacy do you want to build?" he often asked, helping them connect their passions to a greater purpose.

Step 8: Reflecting on the Legacy

Every few months, David initiated a family meeting to reflect on their growth. They'd discuss what they were proud of and how they could improve. During one of these conversations, Jordan said, "I want to teach my kids about connection, like you're teaching us." Emma nodded in agreement, adding, "I want to write stories about family legacies."

David realized in that moment that his efforts were paying off. By creating intentional rituals, prioritizing time together, and modeling the values he cherished, he was building a legacy that would live on through Emma and Jordan. It wasn't just about the memories they shared—it was about the lessons they carried forward, shaping a future grounded in connection and love.

Creating a legacy of love and connection is a conscious, ongoing process. Each memory and moment becomes a part of the foundation you leave behind, shaping how you'll be remembered by those who matter most.

NO MORE DANCING

Legacy in Business: Lessons from Impactful Companies

Legacy isn't just about individuals—it's also about the companies and organizations that leave lasting impressions. Some businesses go beyond profits, shaping cultures, inspiring loyalty, and making a deep impact on both employees and consumers. The question is, what do these companies do differently?

Companies That Built Legacies

1. **Apple: The Power of Innovation and Vision**

    Apple's legacy is not just about technology; it's about a philosophy of innovation and design. Steve Jobs didn't just build a company—he created a movement. Apple's culture fosters creativity, prioritizes user experience, and challenges the status quo. Employees are encouraged to "think different," and customers don't just buy products; they buy into a lifestyle.

    Takeaway for Leaders: How can you encourage innovation within your team? Are you creating an environment where employees feel empowered to think outside the box? Legacy in leadership means cultivating a culture that values forward-thinking ideas and making an impact beyond the bottom line.

2. **Disney: The Legacy of Storytelling and Experience**

    Walt Disney's vision was to create a place where imagination and reality merge. Decades later, Disney remains synonymous with magic, not just because of its films but because of the experience it provides. From theme parks to customer service, Disney employees (or "cast members") are trained to create memorable interactions.

Takeaway for Leaders: How do you create meaningful experiences for your employees and customers? Whether it's through thoughtful onboarding, company traditions, or personalized customer service, every interaction shapes your organization's legacy.

3. **Nike: The Power of Purpose**

   Nike's brand is more than shoes—it's a movement. The company's "Just Do It" slogan speaks to perseverance and excellence. Beyond marketing, Nike takes social stands, supports athletes, and promotes a culture of empowerment. By aligning itself with powerful narratives, Nike has built a brand that represents resilience and aspiration.

   Takeaway for Leaders: Are you standing for something beyond your product or service? Employees and customers are drawn to companies with clear values. Align your leadership with a bigger mission that inspires those around you.

4. **Patagonia: The Legacy of Responsibility**

   Patagonia has become a gold standard in corporate responsibility. The company doesn't just sell outdoor gear—it promotes sustainability, ethical supply chains, and environmental activism. The company's dedication to environmental protection has resulted in deep customer loyalty and a reputation as a business that truly embodies its values.

Takeaway for Leaders: How can your organization contribute to a cause greater than itself? Whether through ethical business practices, corporate social responsibility, or community initiatives, companies that make a difference create legacies that extend far beyond profits.

5. **Zappos: The Legacy of Company Culture**

    Zappos built its brand on customer service and employee happiness. CEO Tony Hsieh created a workplace culture centered around joy, autonomy, and purpose. Employees are encouraged to be themselves, and customers experience a level of care that goes beyond transactions.

    Takeaway for Leaders: Your company's culture is your legacy. Are you fostering an environment where employees feel valued and engaged? Simple things—celebrating wins, prioritizing well-being, and encouraging authenticity—create an atmosphere where people thrive.

Applying These Lessons as a Leader

Whether you're a manager, team lead, or entrepreneur, your leadership style shapes the legacy of your organization. Here are three ways you can incorporate these lessons into your own leadership:

1. **Be Intentional About Culture**
   - Foster an environment where people feel heard and valued.
   - Celebrate small wins and moments of connection within your team.
   - Define and reinforce company values through action, not just words.
2. **Prioritize People Over Profits**
   - Invest in employee development and well-being.
   - Create experiences that make employees and customers feel connected to a larger purpose.
   - Recognize and reward contributions in meaningful ways.
3. **Lead with Vision and Purpose**
   - Challenge your team to think bigger and innovate.
   - Align company goals with a greater mission that resonates beyond business.
   - Be the example—your leadership sets the standard for the legacy your organization will leave behind.

Just like personal legacy, corporate legacy is built in the small, intentional moments. Whether it's a kind word to an employee, an opportunity for growth, or a commitment to excellence, these moments add up—creating a workplace that people remember, respect, and carry forward long after you're gone.

CHAPTER EIGHT

Conclusion: Embracing the Power of Restorative Living

As we reach the end of this journey, it's clear that living restoratively is more than a choice—it's a commitment to a life that values presence, empathy, and connection. No More Dancing has been about shedding the masks, silencing the performative steps, and embracing a way of life that doesn't shy away from pain, vulnerability, or growth. It's about choosing to create meaningful connections, to honor our stories, and to hold space for those who matter most.

Throughout these pages, I've reflected on the legacy left by my father—a legacy that taught me the power of simple, shared moments. He may not have lived a life that fit society's ideals, but he lived a life that mattered deeply to me and my siblings. His movie nights, our fierce games on the court, and his determination to be present left me with memories that have shaped my approach to fatherhood, friendship, and purpose. Those memories are my anchor, reminding me that legacy isn't built by accolades or titles but by the moments we create with the people who truly matter.

Now, I pass that legacy forward to my daughter, Thais, in the bike rides we take, the laughter we share, and the stories we tell. I hope that these moments we build together will remain with her long after I'm gone—a reminder that we don't have to dance around what we feel or hide who we are. We can live openly, restore what's broken, and embrace the fullness of life.

Imagine the World Transformed: Future Pacing

Imagine a world where restorative living isn't just a choice made by a few but a shared commitment embraced by all. Picture a world where communities come together with open hearts, where individuals actively seek to understand one another instead of rushing to judgment. In this world, the workplace becomes a space of collaboration rather than competition. Schools become environments where students feel seen, valued, and safe to express themselves. Families no longer shy away from tough conversations but lean into them with grace and understanding.

This transformation is like the moment at the end of a wedding when the entire crowd is on the dance floor. Everyone is moving in harmony, free of pretenses, simply enjoying the shared rhythm. No one is watching from the sidelines or hiding in the shadows. Instead, there's a collective energy that fills the space—a feeling of unity, joy, and belonging.

This is the world restorative living can create. This is a world where the barriers that separate us crumble, to be replaced by bridges of empathy and connection. This isn't some far-off dream.

It's a tangible future, waiting for those courageous enough to take the first step.

The Before and After

Let's take a moment to reflect on the contrast between where we are now and where we can go. The "before" is where many of us currently live: a world marked by avoidance, fear, and disconnection. We dance around our struggles, sidestep conflict, and bury our emotions. In doing so, we deny ourselves the opportunity to grow and to truly connect with others.

But the "after" is a world where we face challenges head-on. Instead of avoiding difficult conversations, we engage in them with compassion. Instead of hiding our true selves, we embrace vulnerability as a strength. The "after" is a world where restorative values guide us, allowing us to transform conflicts into opportunities for growth and relationships into sources of strength.

The journey from "before" to "after" isn't easy, but it is profoundly worth it.

A Challenge for the Journey Ahead

I won't sugarcoat it: adopting restorative practices is not easy. It requires courage to face uncomfortable truths, discipline to break old habits, and humility to admit when we're wrong. The reality is that long-term success demands short-term sacrifices.

But these sacrifices are worth it. The moments of discomfort lead to breakthroughs in connection. The hard conversations pave the way for healing. The self-reflection unlocks a deeper understanding of yourself and others. The growth you'll experience is immeasurable, and the legacy you'll create will ripple far beyond your immediate circle.

So, I challenge you: take this journey. Commit to living restoratively, even when it feels inconvenient or hard. Choose empathy over judgment, connection over isolation, and growth over stagnation. Let this be the moment you decide to embrace the fullness of life, not just for yourself, but for the people and communities around you.

Your Call to Action

The time to act is now. Don't let the lessons of this book remain just words on a page. Take what you've learned and apply it. Start small:

- Have an open, honest conversation with someone you've been avoiding.
- Practice active listening the next time a friend or colleague shares their struggles.
- Offer forgiveness to someone who has hurt you—or ask for forgiveness from someone you've hurt.

Then, expand outward. Bring restorative practices into your community. Advocate for these principles at your workplace, in your schools, and within your families. Share what you've learned with others and invite them to join you on this journey.

This isn't just about creating change for yourself; it's about starting a movement. Together, we can build a culture that prioritizes connection, understanding, and growth.

The Power of a Shared Purpose

Ultimately, restorative living is about more than just individual change—it's about collective transformation. When we embrace these principles, we become part of something larger than ourselves. We contribute to a world where compassion replaces indifference, where listening replaces speaking over one another, and where unity replaces division.

What is your role in this movement? How will you use your unique talents, experiences, and voice to make an impact? Think about the legacy you want to leave behind. Not just for your children or your community, but for the world.

A Legacy of Restoration

The legacy I've shared throughout this book is deeply personal, rooted in the lessons I learned from my father and the memories I'm creating with my daughter. But this isn't just my story—it's ours. We all have the opportunity to create a legacy of restoration.

May your legacy be a testament to a life truly lived: one where you no longer dance around challenges or emotions but stand firmly in the power of restorative living. May it be a life that leaves the world a little more compassionate, a little more understanding, and a lot more whole.

So, as we close this chapter, remember this: the world doesn't change because of a single grand gesture. It changes because of countless small acts of courage, kindness, and connection.

"The dance we've been avoiding, the conflict we've been sidestepping, the words we've held back—all of it has the power to transform us when we finally stop dancing around it. So let's stop. Let's stand in the power of truth, in the courage of vulnerability, and move together toward a future of healing, connection, and restoration."

Go out and be that change. Let the principles of restorative living guide you, and watch as the world around you transforms. The dance floor is open. It's time to stop standing on the sidelines. Step into the rhythm, embrace the power of restoration, and lead the way forward.

Author's Note

Writing *No More Dancing* was undoubtedly the most challenging and transformative experience of my life. This book took me eight long years to craft—years filled with moments of joy, doubt, growth, and heartbreak. When I look at this finished work, I see more than just a book; I see my life's journey, my family's love, and the indelible mark my father left on me. It's both a tribute to him and a gift to anyone seeking meaning, connection, and resilience. This note is for you, the reader, and those who made this journey possible.

NO MORE DANCING

A Journey of Meaning and Honor

From the moment the idea of *No More Dancing* began to form in my mind, I knew it had to be meaningful—not just to me, but to anyone who turned its pages. I was tasked with the challenge of honoring my father's life while also creating something universal, something that resonated deeply with readers. My father's memory was my guiding light. Every word I wrote carried the weight of his legacy, and every decision I made was steeped in the desire to do justice to the lessons he taught me.

This wasn't an easy process. There were days I stared at a blank page, paralyzed by the fear of not getting it right. On other days, I wrote feverishly, as though my father's spirit was sitting beside me, guiding my hand. And then there were the moments of doubt—when I questioned whether I was capable of creating something worthy of him, worthy of my family, and worthy of the readers who would come to this book looking for hope and inspiration.

Melissa: My Anchor

Through it all, my wife, Melissa Timothy, was my anchor. Melissa, this book wouldn't exist without you. You were my accountability partner, my cheerleader, and my constant source of love and support. You believed in me when I couldn't believe in myself. You reminded me of my "why" when I felt lost, and you held me accountable to the vision I set out to achieve. Thank you for loving me for who I am—flaws and all—and for always encouraging me to be the best version of myself. Your unwavering faith in me gave me the strength to keep going, even on the hardest days.

My Mother: The Believer

To my mother, Eva Rosado, you are the reason I have the courage to dream big and the resilience to see those dreams through. You've always believed in me, even when my path was unclear, and you've instilled in me the belief that anything is achievable with hard work and determination. Your love and encouragement have been my bedrock, and I hope this book makes you proud. Thank you for showing me the power of perseverance and for teaching me that challenges are opportunities in disguise.

Jose: The Resilient One

To my brother, Jose Malave, your resilience has been a source of inspiration for me. Watching you pursue your passions and stay true to yourself, no matter what life threw your way, reminded me of the importance of perseverance. You taught me that passion and purpose can carry us through even the darkest times. Thank you for being a constant example of strength and for showing me what it means to never give up.

Nereida: The Grit and Grace

To my sister, Nereida Malave, your grit and grace in honoring our father by changing careers has been nothing short of inspiring. You've shown me that it's never too late to reinvent ourselves and that love and dedication can drive us to achieve incredible things. Thank you for your courage and for reminding me that our father's legacy lives on in the choices we make and the paths we forge.

NO MORE DANCING

Thais: My Light

To my beautiful daughter, Thais Eva Malave, you are the light of my life and the greatest blessing I've ever received. You changed me forever, Thais. Your laughter, curiosity, and boundless love have been my guiding star throughout this journey. This book is, in many ways, for you. It's a testament to the lessons I want to pass on to you and the world I hope you will grow up in. Thank you for teaching me what truly matters and for being my constant source of inspiration.

A Village of Support

Finally, I want to thank everyone who has crossed my path over the past eight years and contributed to this project. Whether you offered words of encouragement, shared your insights, or simply believed in me, your support has been invaluable. To my friends, colleagues, and mentors—thank you for pushing me to think deeper and aim higher. To my readers, thank you for opening your hearts to this story and for allowing my father's memory to live on through you.

A Love Letter

At its core, *No More Dancing* is a love letter to my family. It's a reflection of the lessons we've learned, the struggles we've endured, and the love that binds us together. It's about honoring the past while embracing the future, and it's about finding meaning in the moments that shape us. I hope this book resonates with you, not just as a story, but as a reminder of the power of love, resilience, and connection.

Thank you for taking this journey with me. My deepest hope is that *No More Dancing* inspires you to honor your own story and the people who have shaped it.

With love and gratitude, Carlos J. Malave

Call to Action: Step Into Your Restorative Power

As you close the pages of *No More Dancing*, I invite you to step boldly into the journey ahead. This book isn't just a reflection of my story—it's a call for transformation, for choosing restoration over avoidance, and for leading lives grounded in courage, love, and truth. The insights, lessons, and principles shared here are tools meant to inspire action, foster connection, and rebuild trust in yourself and the communities you touch.

Start with Yourself

Transformation begins within. Reflect on the areas of your life where you may have been "dancing around" difficult truths or avoiding necessary conversations. Ask yourself:

- What boundaries do I need to set to protect my peace and foster healthy relationships?

- What unresolved emotions or experiences have I been suppressing, and how can I begin addressing them?
- How can I create moments of stillness to listen to my inner voice and honor my needs?

Choose one small action to take today. Whether it's journaling, having an honest conversation, or seeking professional support, know that every step you take toward restoration is a step toward freedom.

Build Connection in Your Relationships

Restorative living thrives in connection. Look at your closest relationships—family, friends, colleagues—and consider how you can bring more honesty, empathy, and accountability into these spaces. Start by:

- Practicing active listening: Be fully present and listen without the intent to respond.
- Initiating hard conversations: Use "I" statements to express your feelings and needs while inviting dialogue.
- Offering grace: Understand that we all stumble, but growth comes from choosing repair over resentment.

Remember, building connection takes time, patience, and vulnerability. Each effort strengthens the foundation of your relationships.

Extend Restoration to Your Community

True transformation doesn't stop at personal growth—it ripples outward. Whether you're an educator, a leader, a parent, or a community member, consider how you can champion restorative practices in the spaces you inhabit. Ask yourself:

- How can I create safe spaces for others to feel heard, valued, and supported?
- What role can I play in fostering accountability and growth in my workplace or community?
- Who around me might need encouragement, understanding, or a reminder that they're not alone?

Start small. It might be through hosting a restorative circle at work, leading with empathy in challenging situations, or simply showing up for someone in need.

Celebrate the Journey

Every step you take, no matter how small, deserves recognition. Transformation is a process, not a destination. Celebrate the moments of growth, the repaired relationships, and the courage it takes to live authentically. Remember: You are not alone on this journey. Each choice you make to live restoratively inspires those around you to do the same.

Share the Movement

If *No More Dancing* has inspired or impacted you, I encourage you to share its message with others. Whether it's through conversations, book clubs, or social media, your voice can amplify the power of restorative living. Tag me or share your story with me—I would love to hear how this journey has unfolded in your life.

Together, we can create a world where avoidance gives way to authenticity, disconnection transforms into understanding, and silence is replaced by courageous dialogue. This is your moment to lead, to love, and to live with restorative power.

Your Next Steps

1. Reflect: Take 15 minutes to identify one area of your life where you can start living more restoratively.
2. Act: Commit to one action this week to deepen a connection or address a long-avoided truth.
3. Share: Tell a friend, colleague, or family member about what you've learned and how they can benefit from restorative practices.

Thank you for taking this journey with me. The power to transform your life, relationships, and community is already within you. Let's choose to stop dancing around the truth and start stepping into our restorative power.

With gratitude and hope, Carlos J. Malave

REFLECTIONS IN PICTURES

The Restorative Journey Behind No More Dancing

The following images capture moments, spaces, and people that inspired, shaped, and reflected the journey of restorative living presented in this book.

Restoring Power Through Community

These moments capture the heart of the Restorative Power Program in action at KIPP Texas, where students and I engaged in deep conversations about accountability, healing, and community building. Featured on ABC 13 News, this work highlights the power of dialogue in transforming school culture— shifting from punishment to understanding, from isolation to connection. Through restorative circles, students found their voices, built trust, and led the way in creating a more supportive environment. This is the impact of true restorative work.

NO MORE DANCING

"My father's greatest goal in life was to be the father he never had—and he accomplished that and so much more. He poured his love, wisdom, and strength into me, showing up in ways that shaped my character, my values, and my purpose. Every lesson he taught, every sacrifice he made, and every moment he was present left an imprint on my heart. His love was unwavering, and his impact will live on forever. I am who I am because of him. I love you, Pa."

"As a kid, dancing was my way of bringing joy to others—spinning, moving, and feeling free. But as I grew older, I started dancing for different reasons—dodging difficult conversations, sidestepping my emotions, and moving around my truth. This book is my journey of learning to stand still, face myself, and embrace the rhythm of who I truly am. No more dancing around what matters most."

ACKNOWLEDGMENTS

To the men who shaped me—this book, No More Dancing, carries pieces of each of you within its pages.

To Rob Powell, Tim Maher, and Robert Guirantes—thank you for being present in my early years, holding me accountable, and showing me what it meant to walk with purpose. You stood beside my father in raising me, and I'm forever grateful for the roles you played.

To my coaches in life and in business—Nate Eklund and Arel Moodie—thank you for showing me how to lead with intention, build with strategy, and still maintain balance as a man, a husband, a father, and a creator.

Each of you played a part in my development, and your impact is woven into the man I've become. This book is not only a reflection of my journey but also a tribute to your influence.

REFERENCES

The development of *No More Dancing: Embracing the Power of Restorative Living* was deeply influenced by extensive research, personal experiences, and conversations with mentors, educators, and practitioners. Below are the key references that supported the ideas presented throughout the book:

Books and Publications

- Brown, Brené. *The Gifts of Imperfection: Let Go of Who You Think You're Supposed to Be and Embrace Who You Are.* Hazelden Publishing.
- Sherman, Lawrence W., and Strang, Heather. *Restorative Justice: The Evidence.* The Smith Institute.
- Van Ness, Daniel W., and Strong, Karen Heetderks. *Restoring Justice: An Introduction to Restorative Justice.* Anderson Publishing.

Research Articles and Studies

- Collaborative for Academic, Social, and Emotional Learning (CASEL). Research on restorative practices in educational settings.
- Centers for Disease Control and Prevention (CDC). Reports on Adverse Childhood Experiences (ACEs) and their long-term impact.
- National Center for Education Statistics. Data on disciplinary practices in U.S. schools.
- *Journal of Experimental Criminology*. Studies examining the impact of restorative justice on recidivism rates.

Key Influences and Frameworks

- Indigenous restorative practices, including Māori and Zulu approaches to justice.
- Positive Behavioral Interventions and Supports (PBIS) in educational environments.
- Restorative circles and community-based healing models grounded in empathy and collective accountability.

ABOUT THE AUTHOR

Carlos J. Malave is the author of Translating Your Success and the visionary developer behind the Restorative Power Program. With over a decade of K-12 teaching experience, Carlos has transformed into a dynamic speaker, curriculum developer, and coach, creating tools that empower educators and learners. His Restorative Power Curriculum is implemented in classrooms and organizations across the U.S. and internationally.

Carlos's work fosters perseverance, compassion, and inspiration, earning recognition on ABC 13 News and praise from

Texas legislators in 2018 for advancing legislation to integrate Restorative Practices into public schools. Over the past four years, he has helped curriculum clients generate over $1 million in sales.

He has extensive experience consulting within higher education and specializes in empowering youth to find strength in vulnerability, building resilience, empathy, and purpose. Originally from New York, Carlos now lives in Houston, Texas, with his wife and daughter, continuing to impact education worldwide through innovative curriculum development and coaching.

www.ingramcontent.com/pod-product-compliance
Lightning Source LLC
Chambersburg PA
CBHW020551030426
42337CB00013B/1051